BLUFF ® TO STOCKS & SHARES

ANNE GORDON

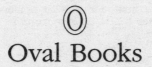

Oval Books

Published by Oval Books
335 Kennington Road
London SE11 4QE
United Kingdom

Telephone: +44 (0)20 7582 7123
Fax: +44 (0)20 7582 1022
E-mail: info@ovalbooks.com
Web site: www.ovalbooks.com

First published by Ravette Publishing, 1998
First published by Oval Books, 1999
Updated 2000, 2002

Series Editor – Anne Tauté

Cover designer – Jim Wire, Quantum
Printer – Cox & Wyman Ltd
Producer – Oval Projects Ltd

Dedicated to David.

The Bluffer's Guides® series is based
on an original idea by Peter Wolfe.

ISBN: 1-902825-64-0

CONTENTS

The Basics   5
  Shares   5
  – Facts of Life   6
  – Dividends   8
  Securities   10
  – Government Bonds   12
  – Valuations   13
  Shares v Securities   15
  Mongrels   16
  – Preference Shares   16
  – Permanent Interest Bearing Shares   16
  – Convertibles   17
  The Stock Market Ball   17

Finding Your Way   19
  Stock Markets   20
  Share Price Services   21
  Indices   25

Buying and Selling   26
  Brand New Shares   26
  Second-hand Stock   32
  Bonds   37

Riding the Ups and Downs   38
  Volatility   38
  Variables   40
  Cover   42

Getting Information   43
  Systems   47

Investing in Exotica 49
   Futures 50
   Options 51
   Futures v Options 53
   Warrants 54
   Foreign Exchange 54
   Swaps 55
   Spread Betting 56

Game Playing 57

Glossary 59

THE BASICS

Understanding stocks and shares is not difficult. If asked to explain the basics you will travel back in time to the Middle Ages when there were three ways of expanding a business:

Method 1: invest more money

Method 2: borrow money

Method 3: become a warlord and terrorise other people into giving you their money

The first two routes have disadvantages, so that over time Method 1 evolved into **shares** (also called **stock**) and Method 2 into **securities**. Shares are simply an efficient way of investing in a business, and securities a way of borrowing. The third technique has fallen into disrepute, although it does still work in Colombia, Moscow and many school playgrounds.

Shares

In the beginning, investors in a business became **partners**, dividing work and profits. They shared each other's money and risks, so if the partnership went bust, all partners were bankrupt. Partnerships were thus a hazardous and inflexible way of doing business.

Companies were a major step forward. A company is an artificial person, with its own legal identity. It is born (or incorporated) and dies (or is liquidated). Just as the human body is built up of cells, so a company is made up of shares. Shareholders own the shares, and therefore own the company and its business. So if you own shares you possess part of the company, though it

5

may only be a tiny part, like a toenail.

Like individuals, companies need money before they can start trading. So shareholders contribute cash, or **inject capital**, into their company in exchange for shares. If things go wrong, their exposure is limited to this capital investment. This is why it is called a 'limited' company. A company is therefore safer than a partnership because shareholders don't risk their homes or their shirts.

The capital is used to run the business. If the company makes a profit, this is usually paid out to the owners as **dividends**. The shareholders can also agree among themselves that part of the profit will be **retained** in the company. If this happens the value of each share grows, producing a **capital gain**.

Sometimes these retained profits are not enough. Perhaps the company wants to buy a roller-blade factory, but hasn't got the money. It can ask its shareholders to contribute more funds in exchange for further shares (a **rights** issue), but if they are unwilling or unable, it may look round for additional investors. It then issues more shares, and sells them to the investors in exchange for their cash. This is called **subscription**. The cash is then used to buy the factory.

Of course, if the factory isn't sufficiently profitable, there will be less money to divide among the bigger group of shareholders. You can thus refer to a new issue of shares as a **dilution**, because the profit-share has been watered down.

Facts of Life

Shares are like sex. You should be capable of gossiping about them. The secret is to sound as if you've heard it all before. We recommend:

- Using aliases. This makes you sound experienced. Shares are **equities** or **stock**. Normal equities are ordinary shares or **common stock**, which distinguishes them from **preference shares** (q.v.) and **deferred shares** (those disqualified from dividends).

- Being provocative. All companies are required to publish an **Annual Report** (like school reports, this is a carefully edited summary of the year's events). Read one that catches your eye, notice who the directors are, and then skim the news. You will soon pick up a salacious titbit that will give the impression you're on the inside track.

- Knowing the big boys. **Blue chips** are the shares of the top companies, and thus the most secure of equity investments. Blue chips are the highest value tokens in US casinos, a reminder that even the safest shares are a gamble.

- Pacing yourself. Because shares are small units, you can keep some and sell some: it's not an all or nothing situation. There is also no need to be faithful to one company – you can hedge your bets by investing in a number of different shares, and disposing of them when they are no longer attractive.

- Ignoring convention. The share's **nominal** (or **par**) **value** is the number on the face of the share: it may be 1p, it may be £1, but is meaningless, like the price on a black-market concert ticket.

- Acknowledging that size does matter. A large holding of shares sells for more than a small holding. A **majority** means you hold enough shares to outvote all other shareholders, appoint the directors and decide how and when to pay out the profits.

- Recognising your power. Like most minorities, small shareholders can cause a lot of trouble. Owning a single share allows you to disrupt **AGMs** (Annual General Meetings), ask awkward questions and get your picture in the papers.

- Planning your next move. If you own 90% or more of a UK company's shares, you can buy out the rest, even if the remaining shareholders don't want to sell. This is allowed by Section 428 of the Companies Act. Dropping a fact like this into a conversation suggests you know an enormous amount about the business world, and may immunise you from sharp practice.

- Plotting your exit. Shares can be sold for cash, making it easy for investors to extract their investment. Withdrawing from a partnership is much messier, and tends to involve hurt feelings.

Dividends

There are two ways to make money from your shares. One is capital growth (when the shares themselves increase in value) and the other is dividends.

Don't be dazzled by dividends. Remember: you and your fellow shareholders already own the company and its profits. A dividend is only a sharing out, or **distribution**, of part or all of that profit to the shareholders which belongs to you whether it is paid out or not. If no dividend is paid, the profits stay in the company. These **retained** profits should mean that the value of each share increases.

The only reasons for preferring dividends to retained earnings (or vice versa) are:

8

- **Tax**. Capital gains may be taxed differently from dividends.

- **Cash flow**. If you require income from your shares, dividends are vital. Otherwise you have to keep selling shares to convert them into cash. This puts you at the mercy of the markets, and exposes you to heavy dealing costs.

Declaring a Dividend

It is normal for companies to pay one dividend a year, based on the annual profits. However it is easy to get muddled, because the dividend is paid in two parts: an **interim dividend**, paid part way through the year and based on expected profits, and a **final dividend**. This cannot be distributed until the shareholders have approved the whole dividend at the AGM.

Another point to watch is that dividends are in pence per share, so depend on the number of shares you have, rather than how much you paid for them. If you have 1000 shares and are due a final dividend of 5p, you will receive a cheque for £50, whether your shares cost a pound or a penny.

Cum and ex

Once a dividend has been declared, the share is **cum-div**: if you buy the share you receive the dividend. But for administrative reasons there has to be a cut-off date after which the shares go **ex-div**, and are marked **xd**. If you buy an ex-div share, the dividend goes to the previous owner. Once a share goes ex-div, it will fall in price, because the dividend value has been stripped out of it. So don't be tempted to buy an ex-div share because it suddenly looks cheap.

Dividend cover

This is the number of times the company could have paid its dividend out of that year's profits. A company with a profit of £10,000 and a dividend of £2,500 has a dividend cover of 4. The higher the cover, the safer the dividend. It implies that the company has plenty of spare money for lean years.

Special dividends

Normally a company pays part of its profits as a dividend and keeps the rest in its reserves to invest in the business. But occasionally the company can't find an economic use for the money it has held back. This is the corporate equivalent of pennies in the piggybank but nothing in the shops. The company therefore gives it back to shareholders as a special dividend.

Share buybacks

An alternative to a special dividend is a share buyback. Instead of returning the cash to shareholders, the company buys its own shares and cancels them. This concentrates the value in the remaining stock, and enhances it.

The company can also use borrowed money to fund a share buyback. If this happens, ask if it is **tax-driven**. This shows you know that interest on debt can often be deducted from pre-tax profits, but that dividends are paid out of post-tax profits. It also demonstrates that you are in the driving seat as far as your investments are concerned.

Securities

If businesses want to borrow, they have a number of options, all unpleasant:

Pawn shops – the borrower is the pawn

Loan sharks – who swallow business assets

Rich friends – but how many people have spare cash?

Banks – parasites on people's savings.

In each case, the lender call the shots. He decides the maximum loan, its repayment date and the rate of interest. Overdraft negotiations always go more smoothly if you recognise this imbalance of power and treat bank managers like a minor deity.

However, one day borrowers rebelled, took control and invented Securities. A security is only a posh word for debt. Other aliases include **bonds**, **debentures** and **loan stock**. Using these terms interchangeably shows that bonds can't tie you in knots.

With a security it is the borrower who fixes the loan amount, the rate of interest and the repayment date. The securities are then snipped into small pieces so lots of smaller savers can buy a slice.

Each slice is a **bond** or IOU. Because individual bonds can be bought and sold, lenders can recover their money by selling the IOUs ahead of the **maturity** date. Like Houdini, bondholders have established their escape route in advance.

Before you get entangled, you should know that:

- They may be secured or unsecured. **Secured** bonds are fastened to an asset owned by the company, such as a building. If the borrower cannot pay, the lender takes the building. An **unsecured** bond has no specific link – lenders are relying on the overall assets of the company to repay the debt. No-one seems deterred by the apparent contradiction of unsecured securities.

- Unlike shares, par values matter for securities – they are the price at which they will be repaid or **mature**. If a bond is sold for less than its par value, it is sold at a **discount**, if for more, at a **premium**.

- Most bonds pay interest, called a **coupon**. Bluffers know that bonds formerly had tear-off coupons which you handed in when claiming interest, like money-off vouchers in Sunday newspapers.

  The coupon may be **fixed** e.g. 10% a year, or it may be floating. A **floating rate** means that the interest rate paid on the bond moves up and down with market rates, like a ship on the tide. Bonds which pay no interest are called **zero coupon bonds** – zeros for short. Zeros are always issued at a discount, so that the seller makes a capital gain when the bond matures, instead of receiving interest.

- If a bond pays interest twice a year in July and January, and you buy it in September, you will also buy the interest which has **accrued** or **rolled up** in the price. This is purchasing **cum-int**. As with shares, for administrative reasons there is a cut-off point near the payout date, and if you buy after this you will receive the bond **ex-int**, i.e. excluding the interest payment.

Bluffers should be aware that bond prices quoted in the press do not include accrued interest, and are thus **clean prices**. To work out what you will actually pay or receive you need to add in the interest, creating a **dirty price**. If you sell at a dirty price just before the ex-div date, collecting the maximum amount of interest as a capital sum, this **bond washing** may get you into hot water with the taxman. Of course, it's a matter of taste who you invite to share your tub.

Government Bonds

Government securities fund the shortfall between a country's income and its expenditure. In the UK, government bonds are called **gilts** – not solid gold, but backed by Bank of England bullion. Buy a gilt, and you buy part of the National Debt.

Other governments have their own bonds – US **treasuries**, German **bunds**, Spanish **bonos** and French **OATS** – commonly sown wild.

Gilts have names – **Treasury**, **Exchequer** and **Funding**, but they could equally well be called Fred or Esmeralda. The names are simply identification tags on the stock register, and have no other purpose.

Dates, in contrast, are very important. Each gilt has a redemption day on which it will be repaid by the government, and these are used to divide gilts into three lengths. Those with a life of less than five years are **shorts**, between five and 15 are **medium-dated**, and more than 15 are **longs**.

Undated gilts will never be repaid and are thus **irredeemable**. War Loan is the best known of these: during the Second World War, people lent their hard-earned savings to the British government, and the money was never repaid. In dangerous times, a government's word may not be its bond.

Valuations

It is easy to make a false move here. Because a security has a redemption value of £100, it would be reasonable to assume it is always worth £100. But this would be wrong. Its value depends upon:

1. **Interest rates**. New bonds have a competitive interest rate – if bank base rates are 7% and

expected to rise, the rate on a 5 year bond may be 9%. However if base rates shoot up to 10% the following year, fresh bonds might be priced at 12%. The market value of the 9% bond will then drop.

Floating Rate Notes (**FRNs**) are immune from rate changes because their interest bobs up and down according to the market. Some FRNs have a **droplock** which fixes the interest if rates fall to a pre-determined level. Droplocks provide extra security for owners, like deadlocks.

2. **Inflation**. If this is high, the money you receive when you redeem your bond will buy considerably less than when you bought it. To eliminate this risk, some gilts and bonds are **index-linked**, so you always recover the **real value** of your investment. If inflation increases by 2% a year, the annual interest on your index-linked bond also grows by 2%. And at the end of the day the lump sum repaid to you also increases by the rate of inflation.

The cost of this protection, or **hedge**, is a lower **nominal** interest rate. For instance, the index-linked gilt to be redeemed in 2020 only carries 2.5% interest – plus the inflation adjustment. Bluffers need to be aware that the inflation measure used for gilts is the **retail price index** – which is based on a basket of goods. You may care to suggest that this is more relevant to supermarkets than stock markets.

3. **Credit ratings**. You should recognise the names of the two main credit-rating agencies – **Standard & Poors**, and **Moody's**. These mark borrowers A-C – scoring triple A for the safest and triple C for the precarious. Their much dreaded inspectors circle the globe, applying continuous assessment and denouncing dunces.

Governments are marked too. If they manage their economy badly, the country's credit rating falls. This affects the value of their securities: existing bonds fall in value and new bonds have to be issued at a higher interest rate to balance the extra risk. This means the government has to spend more to get the same loan from the market.

Credit connoisseurs call very high-risk securities **junk bonds**. These are issued by newcomers or those with poor end of term reports, such as cable TV companies and casinos. Junk bonds give much higher interest rates to compensate for their uncertainties. Although their rates are tempting, remember that, as in any antique shop, apparent bargains may be worthless rubbish.

The value of most bonds is thus a mixture of **price**, **risk**, **interest** and **inflation**. But don't bother balancing these variables. The FT World Bond prices do it for you. Look for the columns headed **Red**, which stands for the **yield to redemption** or the return you can expect to receive on your investment if you buy now and hold to maturity. But frequent checks are needed: a sudden change in yield could turn an encouraging green light to a warning red.

Shares v Securities

There is one question bluffers should never ask, and it is this: "Which are better, shares or securities?" This is like asking whether bread is better than potatoes or football better than rugby. They are different.

If you are asked this question, explain gently that:

1. Shares are more volatile than securities, travelling up and down according to the performance of the

stock market in general and the company in particular. Although the value of securities does move, the movements are less extreme and somewhat more predictable.

2. If the company goes out of business, it is obliged to repay its bondholders before paying shareholders. Securities are thus more secure than shares. On the other hand, if the company does very well, shareholders get the profits, while bondholders only receive their interest payment. So the potential upside of shares is greater, but so is the downside.

3. Investors may want a higher return from shares to compensate for the extra risk. This is the **equity risk premium** (**ERP**). Shares have out-performed bonds in nearly every period of stock-market history, yet no-one regards a demand for ERP as greed.

Mongrels

Mongrels include preference shares, convertibles and PIBs, all of which are part-share, part-security. Unless you intend to be insulting, don't mention **dogs**.

Preference Shares/Preferred Stock

You should always call these **prefs**. Technically shares, prefs look very like securities and their dividends very like interest. Provided the company makes profits, paying pref dividends is compulsory.

But unlike securities, prefs have no set repayment date. However, if the business goes belly-up, prefs have priority (preference) over ordinary shares when the liquidator divides the left-overs.

Permanent Interest Bearing Shares

PIBS should always be referred to by their abbreviation. The full name gives the game away, making your grasp of the subject seem less impressive. PIBS are:

Permanent – in that they can never be redeemed for cash

Interest Bearing – in that they carry a pre-determined rate of interest

Shares – in that they form part of the capital of a building society: owners of PIBS are members of the society.

Convertibles

Convertibles start as securities, paying interest. If conditions improve, they can be switched to equity, receiving the same dividends as other issued shares. But if you miss the deadline for this change, the hood on your convertible slams shut, and you are left clutching a conventional Bond. And as any preacher will tell you, it's risky to rely on a death-bed conversion.

Tips for Stock Market First-Timers

It is not always easy for companies to find someone to buy their shares, or for investors to identify companies in need of extra funds. There are no singles shareholder bars, computer mating services or lonely speculator advertisements.

This is where stock markets come in. By lifting marriage out of the bureaux and on to the dance-floor they make dating easier and more accessible. Their job is to:

a) Regulate the companies who participate.
b) Provide investors with opportunities.
c) Produce information to help you make decisions.

Inside the market willing buyers meet willing sellers, and whispering gossips and glossy magazines swap rumours and sully reputations. At the entrance, bouncers banish those previously convicted of GBH (Guile, Buccaneering and Hanky-panky). But despite these controls, crooks can crash the party, and may bring the house down.

Some days you will find the perfect partner, have fun, and feel on top of the world. On bad days you are left with nothing but a hangover and an empty wallet.

If you want to bluff your way into the ballroom, you need to know the etiquette. Here are a few tips:

- Sophisticated stock market experts will seek you out, and try to seduce you. Don't let this flattery blind you to the dangers involved. The market is always risky, just as marriage is always a lottery.

- Shares and securities are bought and sold (**dealt** or **traded**) on the market. But this is no debutantes' ball – what you buy is mostly second-hand.

- The **timing** of each transaction needs to be watched – good dancers are quick on their feet.

- For every seller there has to be a buyer. Otherwise stocks become wallflowers. Alternatively the price will fall until someone picks it up – perhaps only to cover their position overnight.

- If you blow all your salary in the hopes of having a ball, a sudden market movement can kick you where it hurts.

FINDING YOUR WAY

You can find your way around the markets in three easy steps:

1. Establish your start point

On which national stock exchange is the share or security quoted? Most are only traded in one or two markets. The companies you hear a lot about in the press may be listed in your country, but this is not always the case. Well-known brands may only be quoted in the US.

2. Buy a map

Without maps, even the best bluffers lose their way. We recommend a small scale map, such as a **share price service** with grid references which allow you to locate the performance of each share.

When finding your bearings, remember that not all companies or securities are on the market. Some are too small, some controlling shareholders won't sell to the general public, and yet other companies fail the entry requirements.

In the UK you may be able to buy shares and securities in these **unlisted** companies via the **over-the-counter (OTC)** market. However, as the deals are neither public nor reviewed by **regulators**, a better name might be the 'under-the-counter market'.

3. Compare and contrast

Just as weather men compare Siberian sleet with Hawaiian humidity, you may want to measure your shares against others using **indices**.

1. Stock Markets

There are dozens of stock markets, but you can avoid knowing too much detail by:

1. Prophesying that individual exchanges will soon vaporise into the virtual reality of an internet based global market.

2. Focusing on the big three: **New York**, **London** and **Tokyo**. This shows you appreciate where the real money is. If anyone calls your bluff, remind them that the whole of the Moscow stock market is worth less than a single leading US blue chip.

3. Remembering **Euronext**. This was created in 2001 by the merger of the exchanges in Paris, Brussels and Amsterdam. By the end of that year it traded 1.6 thousand billion euros worth of stock on its electronic exchange; in early 2002 it successfully swallowed the UK futures exchange, LIFFE (pronounced 'life'), so providing LIFFE with an afterlife and securing its future.

4. Being nonchalant about other new markets. These have sprung up in many developing countries, but are little more than political propaganda – a public statement that the national economy is an emerging market of untapped wealth, not a third world basket case.

    Although foreigners flock to seek their fortunes from these legal lotteries, bluffers should either:

    a) Keep away, which allows you to be scathing about the lack of information and regulation;
    b) Recognise them as the market equivalent of an outside chance. This remains true even if your broker suggests Thailand is now favourite to win.

5. **Scattering acronyms.** This is the bluffer's equivalent of name-dropping. It should be carried out casually and with complete confidence. Good examples include:

NYSE – The **New York Stock Exchange**. This should be referred to as 'Wall Street', or, if you wish to demonstrate comfortable informality, as 'the Street'. It is unwise to criticise the way things are done in New York; it is usually only a matter of time before London and others follow suit.

NASDAQ. You will score points for knowing that this stands for the National Association of Securities Dealers Automated Quotation system. It is the second largest US Exchange after Wall Street, and the fourth largest in the world.

AMEX – The **American Stock Exchange**, but without the gold cards.

LSE – The **London Stock Exchange**. This calls itself the main market but it may be toppled from its pedestal if a merger takes place.

AIM. The **Alternative Investment Market**, a UK stock exchange made up of small, ambitious companies is aiming for the main market. The trick is to distinguish rising stars from the more numerous shooting stars which will miss their target.

2. Share Price Services

All bluffers should be able to strip a share price service to its bare essentials without fumbling. This is how:

1. Buy the financial journal relating to that country. In the UK this is the *Financial Times*, in the US the *Wall Street Journal*. Other things being equal, we recommend the *FT*, because of its distinctive colour. Carried under the arm, left open on a chair, even discarded in the office bin, the *FT* is an outward sign that you are in the pink.

   Some markets, such as Brazil or China, are in any event so small that you are better off relying on the world stock market pages of the *FT* or the *Wall Street Journal*. This also saves having to learn Portuguese or Mandarin.

2. Next, review your journal to discover how the shares are analysed. *FT* readers should note that everything is back to front – as discerning bluffers have always suspected. The previous day's play is reviewed on the back page of its Companies and Markets section and then, working inwards, it sets out share prices for all the main listed stocks.

3. Establish the company's business before you search for its share price because companies are not divided alphabetically, but by industry group. If you can't find your company, look in the ragbags: 'Diversified Industrials' and 'Support Services'. Collecting similar shares together in this way allows you to make comparisons, so you know whether to blame the directors for falling behind the competition, or yourself for buying into a sickly sector.

4. Once you have found your share, run your finger along the line and look at the numbers. The first, in bold, gives the price of the stock. Don't expect to buy or sell your shares for exactly this amount, because:

a) it is yesterday's price.
b) it is the mid-point between the selling price and the buying price. (The difference is the dealer's profit.)
c) a number of other factors will affect the amount of cash you receive, such as the size of the deal, commission and stamp duty.

5. The second column shows the price change for that share over the last 24 hours. The third gives you the highest and lowest price in the last year. These put today's price into context.

6. This is followed by a column headed **Volume**, which stands for the number of deals done in that company's shares the previous day.

7. The next column gives the **yield** (**Yld**) on the shares. This is the dividend divided by the market price, or, less technically, the amount of dividend you get for your money. Although a high yield looks like good news, it may reflect higher risk. Tobacco shares often have a yield twice as high as the market average, reflecting the fact that they may damage your financial health.

8. Then comes the **P/E** workout. This is the best indicator of the physical health of your stock. It divides **price** by **earnings per share**. Earnings means profits – and since most companies only dividend out part of their profits, earnings are higher than dividends.

   If two companies have the same share price and the same profit, their P/E is the same. But if one pays a £2 dividend and the other 2p, the first has a very high yield, the second a very low one. In general you should prefer P/E to yield, because dividends are optional.*

The P/E quoted in the *FT* is 'historic', meaning that it is based on numbers in the published accounts. It is worth knowing that most analysts use forward PE ratios, based on forecast profits and an estimated future share price.

If you browse further back through the paper you will find pages for **World Stock Markets**, which gives you much the same information on key foreign stocks as the previous two pages on the London market, except more closely typeset.

Behind that again are several pages of **Managed Funds** – groups of shares, managed as one fund. Instead of buying stock directly, you buy units in a fund, and the fund buys the shares. Insurance companies, pension funds and unit trusts are all managed funds – though not necessarily well-managed.

Currency movements come next. These are important in themselves and also because they affect share prices.

Last is **World Bond Prices**, with information on all gilts and some bonds.

If this probing examination of your affairs leaves you sleepless, hook up to the **internet**. World markets are always awake. You can hang on the web until dawn, watching tiny price movements and waiting to trap deals.

---

* Don't demonstrate steps 4-8 on Mondays, or your bluff will be unmasked. Because there is no trading at weekends, Monday's *FT* summarises the previous week's movements and dividends instead.

3. Indices

Indices measure companies against others. A movement in an index is measured in **points**. You will score some yourself for saying they are meaningless and should be replaced by percentages.

'Beating the index' is the passion of fund managers, but beware: failed managers become whipping boys. Specialist fund managers may invent their own index, and then find it curiously easy to beat. You can thus dismiss the more exotic indices as the toys of spoiled fund managers, and concentrate on a few key benchmarks:

- **The FTSE Actuaries All-Share Index**, known as the 'All-Share', is the most complete UK index. It includes over 900 companies – around 98% of all those on the market.

- **The FTSE 100-Share Index** with which you should be on first name terms, calling it the **FTSE** or **Footsie Index**. This reflects the price movements of the 100 largest UK quoted companies, and because it contains fewer companies than the All-Share, it can be calculated more quickly, allowing you to play Footsie several times a day.

- **The Mid-250**. As with the Premier League, there is intense competition to stay in the Footsie, and relegation to the Mid-250 is a disgrace.

- **The FTSE 350** adds together the 250 and 100, while the **SmallCap** mops up the next 500. Really baby companies nest in the **Fledgling Index**.

Other stock markets have their own indices – the **Hang Seng** in Hong Kong, **Dow Jones** in the US, and **Nikkei** in Japan. Poland has the **Wig** index – so called because its volatility makes your hair fall out.

BUYING AND SELLING

Buying your first shares is like losing your virginity. It is nerve-wracking, quicker than you expected and stands a small chance of being brilliant. But nothing will ever be quite the same again.

Here are the facts of shareholder life.

Brand New Shares

There are three ways of acquiring newly-minted shares – by **Subscription**, **Rights** or **Bonuses**.

1. Subscription

When the market is going well, you will see lots of companies seeking to launch or **float** on the market; and this is usually your first chance to buy the shares. So if you spot a new company with a world-beating innovation – such as spectacles giving you eyes in the back of your head – you may want to **subscribe** for this **new issue**.

The first step is to ask for a **prospectus**. This gives information about the new company, including a **profits forecast**. Bluffers should note that it is very humiliating for a company to fail to meet its profits forecast, and it is therefore likely to be an underestimate. But remember the rest of the market knows this too and will make the same assumption when deciding whether to subscribe for the shares.

The new issue may be priced in advance, using the expected profits and the price of similar companies already on the stock market. You then offer to buy a fixed number of shares at that price. If you think the price is too low, so that it will rapidly increase when the share comes to market, consider **stagging** the issue. This means asking for more shares than you really want, and selling them instantly for a quick profit.

Stagging used to be a risky but rewarding method of gambling on the markets because companies only required full payment for the shares after they were allocated. **Stags** could thus acquire shares and sell them immediately at a profit, without needing to dig very deeply into their own pockets. But because many companies now require full payment on subscription, stagging has become much less fun.

Sometimes it is difficult to fix a share price in advance – there may be no similar listed shares, for example. Then a company makes a **tender offer** – not a gentle introduction to the stock market, but an invitation to guess the price at which the shares will be sold. This is rather like an auction with sealed bids, and, as with an auction, there is usually a reserve price – a minimum which the company will consider.

Having received all the offers, the company fixes the **striking price**. Anyone whose offer was at or above this will receive shares for this price, even if they bid higher. Those who underbid get nothing.

Allocation and Part-payment

If the demand for shares exceeds supply, the issue is **oversubscribed**. The directors then have to work out how to **allocate** or **allot** the shares among the eager investors.

There are many possible recipes. The company could use a simple percentage basis, so that everyone receives 50% of the amount they applied for, or it could ballot the applicants, with the winners securing the prize – though at least the runners-up get their stake back, which is one-up on most lotteries.

In many UK privatisations, priority was given to small investors, who received all the shares they requested. Those applying for large numbers of shares had their applications either scaled down or completely rejected. This approach also deterred **stagging**, as the speculator risked obtaining only a very small number of shares, in exchange for a large subscription payment.

Some stags attempted to circumvent this by **multiple applications**, encouraging their friends or children to apply, or using false names and addresses. However, the government declared open season, and some were caught and prosecuted.

Stags at bay can escape down two other speculative avenues:

- Buying **part-paid shares**. Some new issues, such as the flotation of British Rail, are paid for in two stages. This requires less cash up-front, and so encourages small investors to buy. The advantage for speculators is that part-paid shares are highly geared: if you have paid only half the cost, and the shares increase by 10%, you have a 20% return on your investment. But the opposite is also true – a fall in the share price puts a bigger dent in your return.

- Trading on the **grey markets** – or selling shares in a new company before they are formally listed. Although only a distant cousin of black markets, grey markets can be just as risky because:

  a) If you don't receive all the shares you applied for, you will have sold what you haven't got. Ashen-faced investors have to make up their shortfall by buying when the market opens.

b) You are gambling that the grey market price will be higher than that reached in open trading. If you are wrong, you lose.

Underwriting

It is also possible for shares to be **under-subscribed** – if the issue was priced before a general market fall, for example, or if bad news about the company hits the press. To insulate the company from this risk, new issues are generally **underwritten**. City institutions, mostly merchant banks, agree to buy any shares which the public don't want. In return the company pays the underwriter a fee, rather like paying an insurance premium.

But just as houses are sometimes flooded, burgled or fall down, new issues can **flop**, and the company then calls on its underwriter to buy the shares. The excess stock may 'overhang the market' as underwriters seek to sell it. If this causes a further slide in the share price, you can either hang on and wait for the landslip to stabilise, or clear out in case there's an avalanche.

Placings

Some companies use inaccessible flotation methods. A common example is a **placing**, when shares are disposed of privately to a number of big investors, such as banks or pension funds. You only have a chance to purchase these shares after the flotation, by buying them on the market like any other share.

Privatisations

Jaundiced bluffers who missed the lucrative UK privatisations can condemn them as a reverse Robin

Hood: the government sold public assets to the rich at ridiculous prices.

But when assessing the next privatisation, remember that a sell-off is not by definition a bargain. The shares must be undervalued, and will be if the following have been underestimated:

- assets, such as railway rolling stock
- cost-savings created by more efficient management
- extra profits for which there was previously no incentive.

Demutualisations

No bluffer can ignore the demutualisation bandwagon, piled high with carpetbaggers. Originally building societies and insurance companies were **mutual** organisations. In a mutual, savers and policyholders are the equivalent of shareholders: they are the members of the organisation, and any profits belong to them. In practice mutuals did not make great efforts to distribute profits to its members – a useful definition of a mutual is an 'organisation run for the benefit of management'.

Demutualising means listing the company on the stock market, so its shares can be bought and sold like any other. The most common reason given for demutualising is that the company will obtain access to capital, allowing it to grow and compete, and thus provide its members with better value. But you can be justifiably cynical here and point out that the division of profits between shareholders and savers/ policyholders has to mean that you will get less.

In order to prevent such awkward questions, demutualising companies pay bribes, known as **bonuses**, to their members. These are of course only a share of the society's profits, so they already belong to you. But the money is locked up in the society, and it usually takes a demutualisation to release it. Although some committed mutuals are now passing profits to savers and borrowers in the form of better rates, most people prefer bonuses in the hand to benefits in the bush.

2. Rights

If a company wants to issue more shares, it is only fair that these be offered first to the existing owners. This gives you the opportunity to buy the extra shares needed to keep your percentage holding in the company unchanged. This is known as a **rights issue**, because you have the right to buy the shares before outsiders.

If you decide not to buy, the shares are offered to the public. Although you have saved money, the decision still costs you. You now own a smaller percentage of the company and the value of each of your shares falls.

To encourage existing shareholders to take up their rights, new shares are frequently priced at a discount to the current market value. Although this looks like a bargain, it is a bluff. Remember you cannot buy what you already own – you are not buying more shares cheaply, you are contributing extra capital into the company.

Rights have a value independent of the shares, because they entitle the owner to buy stock at a discount. So if you don't want to exercise your rights, sell them instead of simply allowing them to **lapse**. Timing is crucial here: a fall in the market price makes the rights worthless and evaporates your discount.

After a rights issue has been declared, existing shares are sold with this right attached. This is called **cum-rights**. But because issuing new shares takes time, there is a cut-off day. After that the shares are sold **ex-rights** and the rights stay with the seller. So take care, if a share price you have been tracking suddenly falls – if there is an **xr** next to it, you may not be getting the bargain you expected. The same is true of **xc**, which means ex-capitalisation, a posh term for bonus shares.

3. Bonuses

Bonus shares are also a bluff. Companies may give you bonus shares instead of dividends. But as you already own the company and its profits, a bonus share is not a windfall gain – it is simply a distribution of the profits which already belong to you. Mentioning that a 'bonus' is a misrepresentation gives you street cred with market traders.

There is an exception to this rule. If new shareholders are given bonus shares to reward them for keeping their ordinary shares for a minimum period, they will increase their stake at the expense of people who bought later on the market. This type of bonus share was allotted in some UK privatisations, to encourage Britain to convert from a nation of shopkeepers into a nation of stock-keepers.

Second-hand Stock

Flotations, rights and bonuses all generate brand new equities, but 99% of share dealings involve second-hand stock. This can be worrying. Why would anyone want to sell next year's top-performing equity? You think your shares have reached their peak, but the buyer clearly doesn't agree. The market is a sweepstake, and only one of you has picked the right horse.

Dealing

Stock exchanges are regulated, so you cannot normally buy shares directly from the seller. You have to use an intermediary.

Fortunately, stock exchange intermediaries are approved and inspected, making it less likely that they will run off with your purchase money or sell you shares at yesterday's pre-crash prices – the broker equivalent of clocking cars.

There are broadly two types of intermediary:

1. Those who give you tips.
2. Those who don't.

If you want advice, call a **stockbroker**. If you know your own mind, use an 'execution only' route, such as a high street **shareshop** or a **telephone/ internet dealing system** or web. Some advisers offer both routes: tailor-made and DIY. The former is predictably more expensive than execution-only, but may prevent you signing death warrants on your best shares.

Because your dealer will deal for you, you don't need to understand dealing methods before you can buy and sell shares, any more than you need to know how the internal combustion engine works before you learn to drive.

On the other hand, when talking to a financial adviser, being able to deploy a few choice phrases will give the impression that you are familiar with the mechanics and will notice if you are being taken for a ride. And hinting that you are a habitué of city dealing rooms may mean you get better service.

Shares are sold through one of two systems: **order-driven** and **quote-driven**. In the UK, order-driven trading was initially limited to FTSE 100 shares, and then spread gradually through the next 250. Quote-driven trading survives for the remainder.

Order-driven trading

Under order-driven trading, your broker enters the shares you want to sell on a computer screen, and waits for someone to buy them – i.e. to 'match the order'. However if you have only a few shares, they have to be bundled together with other small deals until they become a big deal. Responsibility for this deal collecting lies with **retail services providers (RSPs)**.

Although the new system is supposed to be cheaper than the old, small investors may find dealing more expensive, because the RSPs can charge extra fees for small volumes and slow turn-around times. It has to be made to be worth their while to deal with you.

Bluffers should always call the introduction of order-driven trading 'Big Bang 2'. The primal 'Big Bang' occurred in October 1986, when a deregulation bomb under the London Stock Market exploded, blowing the closed shop wide open.

Quote-driven trading

This system is run by **market-makers** who generally belong to big **securities houses**, such as ING-Barings. Most of these are international, buying and selling stock in the Far East, Europe and the US, either for big clients, or on their own account. The sun never sets on securities houses, though they sometimes fall under a cloud.

It is the market-makers' prerogative to state the price at which they would be prepared to buy or sell your shares, and the rest of the world decides whether to deal at that price. They quote one price for buying stock and another for selling. The difference between the two is profit, or **spread**. A wide spread fattens their bank balance and creams yours; a narrow spread indicates belt-tightening.

34

If a market-maker deals in a particular stock, he has to trade if requested, even if there is no counter-party to complete the deal. He may thus be caught out with his position **uncovered**, which is both embarrassing and expensive. Market-makers will try to **lay off** this risk, for instance by using a **derivative** (q.v.). It is easier but unacceptable to foist the unwanted stock on to one of the firm's clients. If caught by **Compliance**, it is the market-maker who will be laid off.

In practice only millionaires use market-makers directly. Bluffers use brokers for quote-driven as well as order-driven stock. In the former system, the broker checks the price at which the market-makers are prepared to buy or sell, and selects the most appropriate. He is required by the regulators to deal at 'best execution', so he can't make a killing by taking the best price himself and offering you a less good one.

One thing to watch with the quote-driven system is **normal market size** (**NMS**). This is the maximum deal market-makers are obliged to accept. So if you want to sell your shares, you may find that you can only sell them in small parcels. The count can fall as low as 50 for small company shares, making it difficult to withdraw in a hurry.

Placing Your Order

First check the most recent market price, using the *FT*, teletext or internet. Then, if you are kept in a phone queue while your broker is having lunch, at least you know the profits will cover your phone bill.

If you are using the order-driven system, don't be bluffed into selling 'at best' – i.e. placing the shares you want to buy or sell on the **order book** and waiting for someone to match your offer. At best this is risky, at worst it is dangerous. Once 'on the book', the deal will be settled automatically if someone accepts. Placing no reserve price on the shares is like offering to sell your car to the first person who turns up. On the stock markets you risk having your order met by a **snake in the grass**, who places a ridiculous bid and closes the deal.

Instead, place a **limit order**. This means stating your selling price and waiting for someone to match it. Limit orders allow you to catch a short term movement, a sudden rise or dive, which might otherwise pass unnoticed. Alternatively, ask that your order be carried out only if a perfect match already exists on the order book: this is **fill or kill**. If a partial match is acceptable, you want **execute** or **eliminate**.

Similar rules apply to the quote-driven system. It is always better to give your broker a maximum (buying) or minimum (selling) price rather than leaving it to him to choose when to buy or sell.

Share Certificates

You will not necessarily have a share certificate. The introduction of **Crest**, the Stock Exchange's electronic settlement system, caused the **dematerialisation** of the old paper-based procedure. Many shares are now owned via brokers' **nominee companies**. These are favoured by some because Crest imposes very tight time limits on **settlement** (sorting out the paperwork). So a postal strike or mislaid certificate can submerge your deal. A nominee company will deal more quickly and might also get a better price.

The disadvantage of nominee companies is that you are not listed on the **share register**, and so are marked absent when directors distribute free perks, such as cruises and crystal glasses. In a falling market these titbits can perk you up no end.

Don't Forget

- The **commission** to be charged on the deal. Costs swallow small successes.

- The **tax** consequences of your sale. Planning before dealing trims the taxman's take.

Bonds

It is possible to buy brand-new securities. The UK Government advertises each issue of gilts in the press, and you can cut out the form and send it off with a cheque. But this is the exception. Most new securities are placed with City institutions rather than being sold directly to the public.

You are more likely to be offered second-hand gilts and bonds. These can be traded through brokers, just like shares. For gilts the broker has a special settlement system called CGO2, which allows you to state your dealing price and the number you want to deal.

In the UK you can find an alternative round the corner at your neighbourhood Post Office. This has two benefits:

a) it is cheaper
b) you support the survival of the village shop.

The disadvantage of this method is that you will deal blind as you cannot specify the price at which you wish to buy or sell. If the market moves after you have posted your order, but before it is processed, you may not get the deal you expected.

RIDING THE UPS AND DOWNS

Like time and toddlers, markets don't stand still. They bounce, plunge, rally, slump, advance, wobble and tumble. You can use almost any verb to describe market movements, and the more colourful the better. Shares also harden and become firmer as they move up, and collapse or soften when they fall.

No-one understands market movements, except in retrospect. So bluffers only need to:

1. Describe the day's **volatility**
2. List a few underlying **variables**, and
3. Know how to take **cover**.

1. Volatility

The markets make perfect sense once you accept that they are managed by a manic-depressive. When he's unhappy, shares are virtually given away; when he's euphoric, stock values inflate like balloons. The dot.com delirium is a good example of the latter.

Although this volatility can be disconcerting, don't let it show. Referring to the markets as a 'trillion dollar yo-yo' achieves the right sort of effect.

Bulls and Bears

A rising market is a **bull market** and a falling one a **bear market**. You could describe an extreme bear market as a polar low. At the opposite extreme, markets overheat. Investors become feverish and dizzy, classic signs of vertigo.

Optimists believe a continuing bull market can be sustained by the **goldilocks effect** – keeping bears at bay using low inflation, high growth and plenty of porridge. Pessimists say this is a cock and bull story.

Market Cycles

Charles Dow suggested that market volatility followed a four-stroke cycle:

1. Recovery, led by those who see the bull coming ahead of the herd.

2. Fund managers and camp followers jump on the bandwagon.

3. The world, his wife and their lover all want shares. This is the time to watch out. The Kennedy clan owe their wealth to selling up three weeks before the great crash of 1929 – they were alarmed when their shoeshine boy passed on a market tip. Similarly, when asked how he accumulated his fortune, Baron Rothschild replied, "I sold too soon".

4. Some prick bursts the bubble.

As well as this longer-term cycle there are short term ups and downs. These are often exaggerated, especially in times of **thin trading** such as August. Fund managers have holidays too.

Betas

Differences in the volatility of individual shares are measured by **betas**. A beta of 2 means the share is twice as volatile as the market as a whole. Given the uncertainly surrounding shares generally, bluffers can afford to be fairly sceptical about betas – though when stock values suddenly plummet, they help you avoid a heart attack. Better betas than beta-blockers.

Crashes

Everyone believes they will cash in before the crash. You can dub this delusion the 'superior timing fallacy'.

In reality, no-one knows whether a bad day is a **technical correction**, a dip before the weather brightens up, or the beginning of winter.

Conventional indicators for measuring market movements are of little help. Even when P/E ratios and yields suggest that shares are overvalued and heading for meltdown, the bullish will argue that history is bunk. The problem is that if you come out of the market too soon, you will watch others making hay; stay in too late and your savings will be washed away. But knowing when to sell is as difficult as following a diet based on stopping eating just before you're full.

Cautious investors can frighten their friends by whispering Black Monday, when Wall Street dropped 20% in the day. Shares took five years to crawl back to the same point. The brave will suggest that those who fear market cycles should get on their bikes.

2. Variables

The reason the markets are hard to predict is because there are so many variables. Which will dominate is anyone's guess. Journalists, analysts, bankers and brokers all participate, forecasting tempests, squalls or calm periods. You may also play 'spot the key variable' and win a fortune. It could be any one of the following:

1. The **economies** in which the companies operate. Shares in companies forming part of a healthy, hard-working economy tend to increase in value. Riots, earthquakes and human rights abuses can be bad for markets, especially if they appear on prime time TV.

2. The **industry** of which the company is a part. Some sectors, such as gold mining, are unpredictable, and this instability is reflected in the share price of the

companies involved. Others, like pharmaceuticals and tobacco, are locked into permanent litigation.

3. The **competition** which the company has to face.

4. Sundry **technical effects**. You may be able to gloss over these, but if asked to elaborate, use an example. When Norwich Union joined the stock market in 1997, this increased the number of insurance companies in the FTSE. Many fund managers had to bring their percentage holding in the sector back into line. This drove up the price of similar insurance companies such as Prudential and Royal Sun. Remember that if you can't explain a market movement, you can blame it on technical effects. They are almost impossible to refute and thus form the last refuge of the bluffer.

5. Feelings (called **sentiment** in the markets). As any analyst will tell you, these are fundamental. If everyone you meet is miserable, you are unlikely to be a bundle of laughs yourself. Similarly, a depression in the US infects London and Tokyo, for emotional rather than rational reasons.

6. **Random effects**, which may be real or rumour. Mention the sudden increase in dollar stocks when South Korea was invaded, which subsided equally quickly when the invaders turned out to be four Chinese plane crash survivors. On another occasion, Tokyo dived $5bn in two minutes after UK comedian Lonnie Donegan suffered a heart attack and the Japanese confused his name with Ronnie Reagan's.

7. **Programme trading**. Computer programmes will buy or sell a share once its price reaches a certain point. This has been widely blamed for worsening the Black Monday crash. Once the market fell to a certain point this triggered more programmed

sales, making the market fall further, triggering yet more sales, and so on. Crafty bluffers will present this type of vicious circle as a buying opportunity – once they believe the market has hit rock bottom.

3. Cover

No-one can really control the weather, but you can protect yourself against its worst excesses. The market equivalent of oilskins, Wellington boots and thermal underwear includes:

- Spreading your investments across different stocks and markets. This is based on the fundamental 'don't put all your eggs in one basket' principle of investment, which bluffers should always refer to as "my portfolio management theory".

- Purchasing shares regularly – say once a month. Like most averages, the result is not as good as five A grades, but you won't flunk the exam altogether by bulk-buying at the wrong time. A regular savings scheme run by a unit or investment trust is an easy mechanism for this **pound cost averaging**.

- Staying one step ahead. It is an article of faith that the market anticipates events. If the pound is expected to rise against the dollar, shares which benefit from a stronger pound will increase in value before the pound rises. Get your guess in first and you will move before the market.

- Holding for the long term. This will allow you to ride out temporary ups and downs. Sir John Templeton is the guru of choice here. He said, "The best time to invest is when you have money. This is because history suggests it is not timing which matters, it is time".

GETTING INFORMATION

Information, the raw material for your research, is available from:

1. Banks and Brokers

Merchant banks and large brokers issue advice notes on companies, recommending which shares to buy and sell. These are based on their own enquiries, including meetings with the companies' directors. The quality of these meetings varies: some are simply an opportunity for the company's Board to **talk up** the share price before the directors exercise their share options.

You can afford to be somewhat contemptuous of these opinions, partly because they are self-fulfilling. You may read in the *FT* that 'Associated British Foods fell 10½ to 500p with Dresdner KB said to be negative about the stock'. No-one knows whether the stock fall proves DrKB was correct, or whether the opinion has itself caused the fall.

The other reason to be contemptuous of these advice notes is because you will never be able to take advantage of them. Once you receive the information, it is already too late: the shares will have responded.

2. Company Accounts

If you are interested in a company, you should obtain a copy of its most recent statutory accounts. Many UK listed companies participate in the *FT* **Free Annual Reports Service**. Internet users can contact **CAROL** – not a provider of personal services, but Company Annual Reports On-Line.

Shareholders used to receive full accounts as a

matter of course and right. Regulators have now agreed that only **summary financial statements** need be sent out, rather than the complete Report and Accounts. You should reject this as fiercely as you would an abridged version of a thriller.

Having the proper accounts allows you to play games with numbers. You can calculate:

- **Profit margin**. This is the company's pre-tax profit for the year, divided by its turnover. Turnover of £1m and profits of £100,000 gives a 10% profit margin. So you get 10% of everything you sell. But don't forget that:

  a) You have to share it with the taxman.
  b) Comparisons are odious, unless with companies in the same business. All supermarkets have a higher turnover than advertising agencies.
  c) **Loss-making** companies are not necessarily bad news – patience can be rewarded. Biotechnology companies may make losses for years and then cure the common cold.

- **Gearing, or leverage**. This is the relationship between shareholders' cash and borrowed money. A company with £1m of share capital and £2m of long-term borrowings, perhaps as bonds, will have gearing of 200%. If inadequately geared, a business may have insufficient funds to move forward and so stall on the hard shoulder. On the other hand, if interest rates shoot up, high gearing can cause companies to go to the wall.

- **Asset backing**. It is generally assumed that a company will continue in business, and they are thus valued on a **going concern basis**. However, if you have growing concerns about a company, it is worth reviewing what you would receive if it was wound up and the assets sold. Property companies, for example, have substantial assets; others, like recruitment consultants, are mostly **goodwill**.

However, avoid being lulled into a false sense of security. While it is true that:

a) accounts are audited by an independent accountant who reports on whether they provide a 'true and fair view' of the company's financial position; and

b) accounting standards should be applied even-handedly to the accounts of all companies,

accounting nevertheless remains to some extent a matter of opinion, not to say bluff. And, more relevant still, the annual accounts are usually several months old by the time they are published, so they are already well past their sell-by date.

3. Financial Journalists

Reading the financial press makes you more familiar with the market – and if this doesn't breed contempt, at least it will raise your comfort levels. The cynical will wonder why journalists haven't retired on their profits – or at least joined a merchant bank offering mega-bonuses.

4. Announcements

The stock market requires that listed companies publicise key developments. Sometimes these announcements take investors by surprise – a company may give a **profits warning** that its results will be worse than expected. By the time you hear this the market will already have reacted – your only hope of a quick profit is if you believe it has over-reacted, and buy while stock is cheap.

5. Directors' Dealings

Company directors are privy to secrets affecting the share price, such as boardroom affairs or unexpected takeovers. To prevent them gaining an unfair advantage over the rest of the market, directors of listed companies are not allowed to buy or sell their company's shares at certain sensitive times, such as before the publication of the annual results. This is called a **closed period**.

However they can deal at other times, and significant sales and purchases, especially by more than one director, may indicate that something is up – or down. You, too, can get in on the act because companies have to notify the Stock Exchange within five working days of a director dealing in his company's shares. These transactions appear in the *FT* on a regular basis.

In assessing directors' dealings, ignore **share** (or **stock**) **option** sales. Options give directors the right to buy shares in the company at a cheap price. Usually they have to be held for several years before they can be exercised, and thus act as **golden handcuffs**, keeping key management locked to their jobs. But because the directors will generally need to sell some shares for cash in order to pay the tax on the option arrangement, share option sales do not mean the company is going downhill – unless of course the directors all exercise their options simultaneously and leave to join a competitor.

Systems

Faced with such a profusion of information, many fund managers adopt a **stock-picking system**. You can do the same. There is no need for originality – begging, borrowing and stealing are all acceptable. The only measure of success is profit.

1. Choose a Style

There are two main styles: growth and value. Under the **growth** approach, managers pick stocks with high dividend yields relative to their share price. The **value** method selects shares with lower yields but an expectation of higher capital growth.

In a rising market, growth stocks often succeed on both fronts, creating big performance-related payouts for fund managers. In a declining market, value stocks may fall less sharply than others. Unsurprisingly, few fund managers follow a value style, as they are generally willing to gamble other people's money for the chance of higher bonuses.

A third style is **thematic**. A concept, such as energy or technology, is identified and appropriate companies selected. As philatelists know, thematic collecting is sometimes in vogue, sometimes scorned. But it has never proved as popular or as profitable as picking your own. You can therefore either treat thematic styles with undisguised enthusiasm or with the kind of lofty disdain displayed by mannequins on the cat-walk.

2. Copy a Guru

Every religion has its gurus. The secret is to follow the historically successful, rather than those who simply talk about it. The best are billionaires, but one pundit recently admitted his advice was so poor that you would have done better investing in a building society.

Gurus to look out for include **O'Higgins**. His Rule for investing has reaped rewards in some years, but in others has proved that rules are made to be broken. **Warren Buffett**, one of the richest men in the world, thoroughly researches his investments, looking for undervalued companies. You can quote his remark that, "In the short term the markets are voting machines – in the long term they are weighing machines". This cryptic observation means that the market will eventually evaluate every company correctly, creating profits for those who spot bargains.

There are two problems with imitating gurus, even good ones:

a) They often contradict each other when recommend-ing routes to salvation, so causing confusion. If you want to follow gurus, select one and become his disciple. Never put your faith in an ecumenical approach.
b) Although copying gurus can be enlightening, don't expect to match their success: meditating before breakfast won't turn you into the next Dalai Lama.

3. Follow the Charts

Like meteorologists, market analysts create patterns from the past and use them to predict the future. This is called charting. Sceptics may suggest that astrolog-ical charts would be equally effective.

Enthusiasts can buy a computer charting program, and watch sequences develop on the screen. Key patterns to watch out for include the **head and shoulders**: two small peaks with a larger one in the middle. If you spot this, expect a sharp price fall to follow. Then there are **double bottoms**, when the price bounces twice off the same low point. And the mere mention of **candlestick charting**, **engulfing patterns**, **dark cloud** cover and **spinning tops** is enough to send most brokers running for the safety of an umbrella fund.

Charts should not be confused with models. Computer modelling digests an enormous amount of information and then selects stocks to meet predetermined requirements – such as shares which will move in opposite directions if the pound strengthens. Models thus allow fund managers to manage risk more effectively, though they are rarely an acceptable excuse for working late at the office.

The **Coppock Indicator** combines psychoanalysis with market analysis. The market is a traumatised individual, needing time to recover from bereavement and loss, such as when a cherished investment gives up all signs of life. This emotional reaction is often out of line with reality, and the well-adjusted investor can make a fortune by standing apart from the crowd.

INVESTING IN EXOTICA

Investing in exotica is like emigrating to Tahiti. Few people copy Gauguin and gamble everything on the possibility of paradise. But you should always sound as if you might take the plunge – even though the closest you may get is a two week package holiday in Guernsey.

Most exotica piggyback on, or derive from, real assets, such as shares or commodities. Once you understand this, you have grasped the concept of the

derivative. This is vital, as the term 'derivative' is the bluffer's passport. Use it frequently and with confidence, and it will win you acceptance in the stock market's holy of holies, the City pub.

Futures

The Futures Market is an X-rated, grown-up version of the Saturday market where people buy and sell, not goods, but the contracts to buy and sell goods. If you have the right to buy 100 tons of zinc next year for £1,000 a ton, and a worldwide shortage doubles the price, your right to buy the zinc can itself be traded.

Contracts to sell metals and food are **commodity futures**. Once they took off, the idea spread to other markets. People began to purchase the right to buy shares at some future date: these are **financial futures**.

If you deal in futures you will either be:

a) a risk-taker, gambling for a profit.
b) risk-averse, hedging to cover an exposure you already have.

Guaranteed equity products (q.v.), provide you with a handy example of using derivatives to hedge. The company selling you the GEB invests your money on the markets. This is fine if they go up: it simply sells its investments and gives you your return. But if markets fall, it will be out of pocket because it has guaranteed all or part of your capital. To protect itself from this risk, the company buys a derivative from a dealer, such as a merchant bank. GEBs are an every-day financial product, sold in their millions to arm-chair investors, yet they disguise a derivative. Futures are closer than you think.

Options

You don't need a horse to win money at the races, or shares to make profits on the markets. Options allow you to gamble that a share will go up or down, without having to bother with real equities. This is how it works:

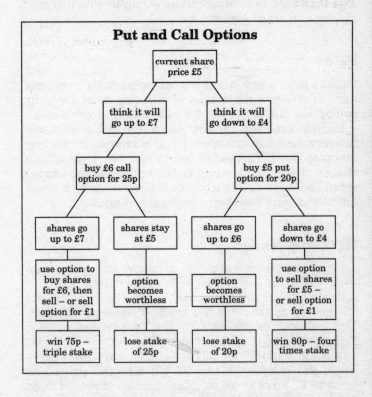

Put and Call Options

- current share price £5
  - think it will go up to £7
    - buy £6 call option for 25p
      - shares go up to £7
        - use option to buy shares for £6, then sell – or sell option for £1
          - win 75p – triple stake
      - shares stay at £5
        - option becomes worthless
          - lose stake of 25p
  - think it will go down to £4
    - buy £5 put option for 20p
      - shares go up to £6
        - option becomes worthless
          - lose stake of 20p
      - shares go down to £4
        - use option to sell shares for £5 – or sell option for £1
          - win 80p – four times stake

NB: a good bluffer knows his options and doesn't muddle calls and puts. Instead he borrows two common abbreviations, **BC** (Buy-Call) and **PS** (Put-Sell).

Straddle

If you are sitting on the fence, and can't decide whether the shares will go up or down, try a **straddle**. This is a gamble that the shares will not sit still – a reasonable assumption given the volatility of the market and how quickly fences become uncomfortable. The **strangle** is a masochistic straddle which comes in long and short versions.

Price

Option prices are a matter of opinion. If everyone expects the price to rise, you will pay a lot for your call option but very little for your put, and vice versa.

Unlike real life, prices generally fall over time. Share values can change a lot in a year, so if you buy an option with 12 months left to run, you have a high chance of winning the bet, so the option will be expensive. The odds are much less if there is only a week left to run, and you might pick up a bargain.

OTC and Traded

An option can be specially designed for you, as an **over-the-counter (OTC)** or bespoke option, which is tailored to your requirements. You can also buy or sell off-the-peg options via the **traded options market**. This allows you to deal in the options themselves rather than buying the underlying shares. So if you had bought 10,000 £6 call options on Paradise shares when the market price was £5, and the price had risen to £7 after three months and was expected to go on rising, you could close out your bet and sell your option at a profit.

Gearing

Options are **highly geared**, so that for a small stake the profits/losses can be considerable. In the summer of 1997 Far Eastern markets fell 5% in two days, and the cost of put options to sell shares in the Hong Kong and Shanghai Bank rose from 3½p to 45p. A £3,500 stake would thus have sky-rocketed in value to £45,000.

Futures v Options

Distinguish your future from your options and you will impress. With an option you have bought a right to choose. If the price isn't right, do nothing and it will disappear. The worst that can happen is that you lose your stake. But with a future you have bought the right to have something delivered.

A satisfactory way of unsettling companies with large derivatives transactions is to ask, "What happens if you have to take delivery?". With commodities, delivery means large warehouses and expensive storage; with shares, delivery involves stamp duty and transaction costs which may wipe out any profit.

Futures are more dangerous than options because only a small deposit is needed to secure delivery. But if it goes wrong, you might not have enough money to meet the obligations you have created. This is what happened to Nick Leeson: the Singapore trader bought and sold these derivatives on an enormous scale, and the markets moved against him.

In the UK, financial futures and options can be traded on the **London International Financial Futures Exchange (LIFFE)**. By December 2001 LIFFE was trading a mind-bending £550 billion a day of futures and options contracts. This is almost 25 times more than the volume of shares traded on the London Stock Exchange.

Warrants

Some new shares have warrants attached. These give shareholders the right to buy more stock in the future at a guaranteed fixed price. The idea is that, in the early years of a company, when profits are low, warrants help arrest shareholders' interest and prevent them from selling up.

Warrants themselves can also be bought and sold. Buying warrants is a way of investing in the stock market at relatively low cost (the warrants cost very much less than the shares) but at much higher risk. For example, in the four year period to 1997, Hanson shares fell by a disappointing 45%, but the company's warrants imploded, losing 99% of their value. So an unwarranted gamble could lose you a fortune.

Foreign Exchange (FOREX)

Just as you can bet on shares and commodities, so you can gamble that sterling will move up against the dollar, or the baht become less desirable than the ringit. You can either:

a) Purchase the currency itself, or
b) Buy a future or option.

A country's currency is like a company's share price. If UK plc is selling excellent products and services, people will need sterling to purchase these goods, and so demand for the currency strengthens.

Another factor is **domestic interest rates**. If the national bank increases its minimum interest rate (the **base rate**), people will buy that currency in order to obtain the higher rate. But there is a limit to this. If the pound is **over-valued** relative to other currencies and people believe its value will soon fall, they won't buy the currency even if the interest rate is high.

The 1992 sterling crisis illustrates this. The British cabinet believed that the pound's value against European currencies was sustainable and kept increasing interest rates to make people buy pounds. Everyone else reckoned it was going to fall. Indeed many currency speculators sold currency they didn't yet have, at the old exchange rate. When sterling fell against the mark by 10%, they were able to buy pounds at the new, lower rate, use these purchases to settle their sales, and make a profit. **George Soros** is the name to conjure with here – he made $1.5bn by this route.

The size of the foreign currency derivatives market is alarming. It is estimated (though no-one knows for sure, so bluffing is very acceptable) that four times the annual US Gross Domestic Product moves through corporate treasuries every month. The whole thing can be seen as an arch-bluff, with promises going round and round in circles.

SWAPS

Don't be intimidated by swaps. Children swap stamps, and barter is older than money. Common swaps include currencies, interest rates, exchanging debt for equity and vice versa.

A simple swap occurs if an English company wants German marks, but has a poor credit rating in

Germany, and a German company wants sterling. The two borrow their own currencies and then swap. They thus get the loans on better terms.

Standing in the middle of the two **counterparties** is usually a bank, taking its cut of the deal. And beyond this simple **plain vanilla swap**, there are more complicated versions: the swaps can themselves be 'on-swapped', or traded on the market.

Each side of a swap is a leg. So if a fixed rate loan is swapped with a floating rate loan, you have a **fixed leg** and a **floating leg**. If you get it wrong, either can give you a nasty kick, but used appropriately you will be one step ahead.

Spread Betting

As well as gambles masquerading as clever financial instruments, it is also possible to bet directly. If you think the market will go down 200 points next month but the general view is that it will go up, you can place a bet with a financial bookmaker. For each point it drops below the expected level, you will win. But if it stays the same or goes up, you will lose.

In the UK the advantage of spread betting over derivatives is that profits from gambling are tax free, whereas stocks, shares and derivatives are deemed to be investments – a government bluff which allows the taxman to take a slice of your stock market successes. This is that rare occasion when the winner takes all.

GAME PLAYING

While all market games are risky, some are both risky and illegal. As well as robbers, the market has its own cops or regulators who police the games.

Selling Short

You sell short if you dispose of shares before you buy them – rather like an antiques dealer selling the same table to two different customers, and then having to find an exact copy by ringing round his mates. It is always embarrassing to be caught short, especially in an inconvenient place like an open market.

Selling short is common for market-makers, and prices may rise as they buy more stock to balance their books. Speculators sell short if they expect prices to fall. A tidal wave of speculation may itself cause prices to sink. This is a **bear raid**. The sellers then buy at the lower price to meet their sale obligations and turn a quick profit.

But if the gamble doesn't pay off, and prices rise instead, those who sold short will have to buy at the higher price. Market-makers sometimes give speculators an uncomfortable **bear squeeze**, artificially forcing prices up. The gamblers are then forced to cover their exposed parts in a frenzy of **bear covering**.

Arbitrage

This is carried out by **arbitrageurs** – 'arbs' to the cognoscenti. Arbitrage is possible when a similar item is valued differently in two markets. If American Airlines shares are $5 in the US but $5.10 in Tokyo, you could make a profit by buying in one market and selling in the other.

People also arbitrage between currencies – if dollars are in demand in Hong Kong, but cheap in Mexico, an international securities house may arbitrage between them. This helps form the so-called **perfect market** (q.v.). In practice, it is more common to be told about past perfects than it is to find a future perfect.

Insider Dealing

If the trainer of the Gold Cup favourite gives you a hot tip, bank your winnings. If Sharko's directors tell you they are buying Eelco, and you buy Eelco shares knowing they will go up once the takeover is announced, this is illegal, and perpetrators may go to prison. It is insider dealing and unfair to the other people in the market.

But since rumour is a major market force, it is sometimes only possible to distinguish insider dealing from gossip after the event, when you have cashed in your knowledge – only to have your fortune removed by the regulators, who monitor unusual share dealings.

Since small investors are more likely than others to be hurt by insider dealing, bluffers should vehemently oppose the practice. But in reality you are more likely to be caught by outsider dealing – acting on old gossip already discounted by the market. When Eelco's takeover happens, the shares are static, because the transaction had been widely forecast on trading floors.

Worse still, the tipster may simply be talking up the stock because he holds too much of it. An old stock exchange saying is 'where there's a tip there's a tap' – meaning a large surplus of shares waiting to be off-loaded.

Internet chat-rooms have updated this truth: the shares of a fingerprint identification company tripled in 1996 when rumours on the net suggested it had won government contracts. On some Exchanges, computer surveillance snares sensitive information, hoping to protect investors from these webs of deception.

Greenmail

If a third company, Xtort, builds up a stake in Eelco, and threatens to sell the shares to Sharko, Eelco may be bullied into buying them – and paying more green-backs than Xtort could have obtained in the market-place. Such cowboys are commoner in the US than the UK, where it is more difficult for companies to buy their own shares.

Chinese Walls

Large securities houses carry out a host of market-related functions. A fund manager may look after a client's pension fund, while his/her best friend advises on takeovers. If the two collaborate, the fund manager would have access to insider information, enabling him or her to buy the target's shares in advance. This would improve both the fund performance and the fund manager's own personal bonus.

Leaks of this sort are discouraged by Chinese walls: artificial barriers to prevent information crossing between one department and another. The trouble with any wall is that guards and gatekeepers can be bribed. Even this becomes unnecessary if the wall is covered in a grapevine. Chinese whispers can defeat Chinese walls.

GLOSSARY

Bottom fishing – Scavenging the market's sea-bed for bargain companies.

Cap – Fixing a maximum dealing price. The opposite, a **collar** or **minimum price**, stops you risking your neck when dealing.

Carpetbaggers – Speculators who climb on the magic carpet of mutuality, hoping to bag flotation windfalls.

Cash cow – Business milked for its profits but without growth prospects. The profits are frequently distributed as cream to fat cats.

Common stock – Ordinary shares. Like most commoners, at the back of the queue in hard times: if the company winds up they may receive nothing.

Compliance – Internal regulation of financial firms. Less user-friendly than laxatives.

Dogs – Unattractive, underperforming investments. Definitely not an investor's best friend.

EGM – Extraordinary General Meeting. Any shareholder meeting other than the AGM. Indicates how rarely directors consult the owners.

Financial engineering – Changing one product, such as a fixed interest dollar bond into another, such as a floating rate sterling bond. Better paid than civil engineering, but less polite.

Financial instrument – Catch-all phrase for anything bought and sold on the stock market, including shares, securities, options and futures.

Flop – Failed share issue. Directors take refuge in the dog-house or worse.

FSA – The UK super-regulator. An alternative name might be Regulator and Investor Protection Office (RIPOFF).

Fund Manager – Whiz kid who makes a fortune managing your money.

Going long – Piling up shares. Compare **selling short**.

Golden parachute – Arrangements made by senior executives to ensure a comfortable landing if kicked out when the company balloon goes up.

Goodwill – Intangible part of a company's value. Includes brand name, reputation and quality staff. The term avoids openly recognising the value of employees, so minimising the badwill caused by low salaries.

Kicker – An extra benefit that adds extra lift to a bond. Also known as a **sweetener**.

Maturity – Repayment date for investment. By the time you get the money you are likely to be well-ripened.

M&A – Mergers and Acquisitions. Most merchant banks have M&A departments, peopled by Machiavellian and Arrogant insomniacs.

Nomad – Nominated adviser for an **AIM** company. If he wanders off, it is automatically de-listed.

Peg – Link between one currency and another. The Hong Kong dollar is pegged to the US dollar, so they rise and fall together, like washing on a line.

Penny shares – Low cost shares, so every penny represents a high percentage of the share's value. Bluffers might do better spending their pennies on more public and convenient companies.

Perfect Market Theory (PMT) – Assumption that prices automatically find their correct level. Fitting reality into this theory is more stressful than PMT of the female kind.

Phantom – Pretend shares or options. Key employees are often given them as part of their pay and perks. The phantoms mirror the performance of real shares but, being incorporeal, do not require the same shareholder consents.

Pincs – Two-tier property bond, part rental income, part capital growth. To be distinguished from gay disposable income, or the **pink pound**.

Quote – To be **listed** on the stock market, so the shares or securities can be bought and sold by the general public.

Real – Adjusted for inflation.

Red chips – Chinese-backed companies listed in Hong Kong. More of a capitalist fifth column than a communist blue chip.

Redemption – Date when a security is redeemed. More certain than the version advocated by doorstepping evangelists.

Regulators – State appointed bodies who superintend the financial industry and whose aim, like bran, is to keep everything regular.

Scrip – Bonus shares. Not to be confused with **strip** – separating the dividend or interest element from an underlying asset, such as a football shirt.

Stock lending – Lending shares to someone who needs them, such as an investor who has sold short, for which a small fee is paid.

Stock market – Mythical labyrinth inhabited by bulls, bears, stags, snakes, sharks and jargon.

Stop-loss – Order to sell if the price falls below a certain level, like water triggering a stop-cock.

Suspension – Temporary hang up. Shares and securities are suspended from the market while the headmaster sorts out what has happened. May be a prelude to expulsion.

Tap stock – Newly-issued gilt stored in government vaults, drip-fed into the market to prevent flooding.

Tigers – Burning bright economies – which may be meteors not stars.

Tobin's Q – The relationship between a company's market value and the cost of replacing its assets. If Q is less than 1, the company is vulnerable to a takeover. Qs can be experienced at first hand by dialling a telephone dealing service.

Wall of money – Enormous sums waiting to be invested in the markets. These piles of cash form a stock market crash barrier.

Xa – Ex-all, printed next to a share in the *FT* listing. If you buy xa shares you won't get any of the goodies (bonus, rights or dividends) which attracted you to the shares. It pays to read the very small print.

Zeros – Bonds which pay no interest. Instead they are issued at a discount to face value and you receive the full amount on maturity. The reward thus comes as a lump sum at the end.

THE AUTHOR

The daughter of a property speculator and the granddaughter of a bank manager, Anne Gordon initially trained as a medieval historian, but it was not long before futures seemed more attractive than pasts.

She feels her financial acumen has improved considerably since her first week in the City of London when she astonished herself by realising that 'an invoice' was only a bill.

She moved to Hong Kong just in time for the 1987 stock market crash, and returned to the UK at the time of sterling's withdrawal from the Exchange Rate Mechanism. She insists the two events were purely coincidental. Her whereabouts on Black Monday remain a secret, though she claims to have receipts to show that she was not in New York at the time.

Having decided that it was more exhilarating to look after other people's money than risk her own, she now advises fund managers. Any personal speculation is limited by a predilection for paragliding, a large mortgage, and the most expensive dentist in the world.
